MINDFULNESS AND MOVEMENT FOR CHILDREN

Michele Tryon MA, BS, CCLS
And
Marsha Engle LCSW, M.Ed., RYT

Mindfulness and Movement for Children

By Michele Tryon and Marsha Engle

Thank you to our talented friend for creating The Mindful Living Institute logo, and the posters and illustrations for this curriculum:

Sally Valk
graphic design | illustration | digital photography | printing
sallyvalk757@gmail.com

Mindfulness and Movement
ISBN 978-1522914143
Copyright 2015 Michele Tryon/Marsha Engle
All Rights Reserved
Printed by Createspace
United States of America

Dear Mindfulness and Movement Facilitator,

Thank you for joining us on the mindfulness journey and for your commitment to creating mindful environments where children can grow and thrive. We are certain that you will enhance your own sense of peace and joy in working with children as you engage in the program.

This curriculum will support your efforts and provide a foundation for mindfulness in your group or classroom. The program is designed for young school age children, however the concepts are universal. We encourage you to adjust the program to meet your needs and the needs of your students.

As the lessons are completed remember to reinforce the concept in everyday situations and interactions. The key to becoming mindful is to live it!

Wishing you presence, ease and joy,

Marsha and Michele

Goal and Objective(s)

Goal: To enhance overall well-being and promote optimal development in children, by teaching mindfulness and movement techniques through interaction and play.

Objective(s):

1) To strengthen positive self-concept and self-awareness.
2) To enhance development of emotional self-regulation.
    a. Improve the ability to pay attention.
    b. Improve self-control.
3) To develop the skills needed to engage in positive reciprocal relationship.
    a. Build empathy.
4) To build foundations for whole brain function.
    a. Enhance learning.
    b. Reduce stress and enhance the ability to cope with stress.

Did you know?

- We have 100 billion brain cells – called neurons.
- EACH neuron has an average of 10,000 connections to other neurons, creating trillions upon trillions of connections in the brain.
- Neurons talk to each other through the exchange of chemicals and create neural pathways that become the architecture of the brain.
- The brain also contains mirror neurons. These specialized neurons allow us to understand the actions of others and prime us to imitate the actions of others.
- Mindfulness in children begins with self-regulation and empathy in adults.
- Children are greatly impacted by observing the actions of adults.
- Even before children are able to reason and understand the intention behind another's behavior, they have the capacity to perceive and react.
- The wiring of the brain is negatively impacted by stress and the related chemicals- adrenaline and cortisol.
- Stress chemicals impede learning and memory, and decrease a child's capacity for self-regulation.
- A child's emotional intelligence or E.Q., ability to understand and regulate their own feelings and respond appropriately to the feelings of others, is as important in academic success as their intelligence quotient or I.Q., capacity for cognitive learning.
- Mindfulness decreases stress and enhances the brains ability to focus.
- Children who are calm and connected can better focus and access the executive center of the brain (frontal cortex) allowing conscious positive decision making when faced with everyday challenges.

WHY Mindfulness?

According to the Association for Mindfulness and Education, the past few decades have found that mindfulness training develops: *Increased attention, increased executive function (working memory, planning, organization, impulse control), decreased ADHD behaviors specifically hyperactivity and impulsivity, fewer conduct and anger management problems, increased emotional regulation, increased self-calming, increased social skills and social compliance, increased care for others, decreased negative affect or emotions, decreased anxiety in general and test anxiety in particular, decreased depression, increased sense of calmness, relaxation and self-acceptance, increased self-esteem, increased quality of sleep.* (www.mindfulnessinschools.org)

Due to the results of a meta-analysis of 213 Social Emotional Learning (SEL) programs with 270,000 students that clearly established the effectiveness of such programs in making positive impacts in a number of areas critical to the success of students, legislation is being introduced to support SEL program funding in schools across the Nation.

The Center for Disease Control recommends that schools, "provide students with the academic, emotional, and social skills necessary to be actively engaged in school." There is a critical connection between a feeling of safety and security in schools and a child's ability to learn. http://timryan.house.gov/press-release/congressman-tim-ryan-introduces-academic-social-and-emotional-learning-act-0

WHY Movement?

Thanks to new insights from brain research, we have gained a greater understanding about the importance of body/mind integration in learning and in emotional regulation. No longer can we maintain a learning environment that dictates sitting still and being quiet. Our entire brain structure is intimately connected to and grown by 1) movement and 2) a sense of emotional safety – the experience of being cared about, and feeling important and accepted. Movement and emotional safety play a critical role in the creation of nerve cell networks, the fundamental ground of learning. (Hannaford, 2005)

Table of Content

About the Authors – page 1
Part 1 – Mindfulness
      Session 1 - Monkey Mind- page 2
      Session 2 - Crocodile Chomp-Down - page 4
      Session 3 - Pokey Porcupine - page 6
      Session 4 - Peaceful Porpoise - page 9

Brain-gym ®- PACE activity – page 12

Part 2 – Mindfulness and Movement Tools
      Calming (relaxation) and mind quieting activities – page 13
      Thought stopping – reframing activities – page 15
      Energy release activities – page 17
      Heart Connection activities and closure – page 17
      Yoga Poses – page 23

Optional Mindfulness Props – page 19

Format

The full program is designed to be taught in four (4) sessions.

Teach the lesson in PART 1

AND

Choose a companion MINDFULNESS TOOL from PART 2.

Each session is designed to be taught in either 30, 60 or 90 minutes, depending on your needs and the ages of the children participating.

If the session needs to be shorter in duration, it is recommended that you provide the basic mindfulness concept included in PART 1 and then skip to PART 2 of the curriculum to choose your movement activity.

If lessons are shortened, it will be imperative to reinforce the concepts in daily activities so children can master the material.

The Program is designed for children ages 5-12 and can be adapted for pre-school children. There are notes and suggestions at the end of each session for gearing the lesson to younger children.

About the Authors

Michele Tryon, MA, BS, CCLS is a certified child life specialist who has worked extensively with children, families, and professionals in homes, schools, communities, and hospitals for over 25 years. As a child life specialist Michele has provided psycho-social support to children and families in stressful healthcare situations, and is practiced in using mindfulness techniques to promote coping and decrease trauma. As community outreach coordinator for The Children's Hospital of the King's Daughters in Norfolk, Virginia, Michele conducts programs and collaborates with healthcare, school and community partners to promote best practice in parenting education on a variety of topics, including *mindful parenting* and *conscious discipline*. She is co-author of the *Nurturing Program for Parents and Their Children with Special Needs and Health Challenges* and is a national trainer/consultant for Nurturing Parenting Programs. ™ She is co-chair of the Hampton Roads Parenting Education Network, and a member of the Virginia Statewide Parenting Education Coalition's Best Practice Committee. Michele completed a year-long program in Energy Awareness Training with the Personal Transformation and Courage Institute, has a BS degree in Psychology Child Life from Utica Collage of Syracuse University and a MA degree in Transpersonal Studies from Atlantic University. She co-founded the Mindful Living Institute in 2014.

Marsha Engle, LCSW, M.Ed, RYT is a licensed clinical social worker who has worked to promote the well-being of children and families for many years – first as a special education teacher and later as a counselor working with substance-abusing teens and their families. Marsha has a private psychotherapy practice, where she specializes in treating depression, anxiety, and other emotional disorders with mindfulness techniques. She is a yoga therapist, teaches yoga and meditation, and conducts mindfulness workshops and trainings throughout the state. Marsha earned her undergraduate degree in social work from Virginia Intermont College, her Masters in Special Education from the College of William and Mary, and her Masters in Social Work from Norfolk State University. She co-founded The Mindful Living Institute in 2014.

PART 1- Mindfulness

Session one activity: Monkey Mind

1. Have the children do the PACE Brain-gym® movements and then sit on the floor in a circle. The PACE Brain-gym® movements are detailed in the back of the book with an explanation of the benefits of the movements. Starting the program with Brain-gym® before being seated will foster a greater ability for the children to be present during the session, and decrease distraction and fidgeting. Tell children Brain-gym® makes them calmer and smarter!

2. Hold up the poster of the child on the path.

3. Explain that the child's name is Gia. He is sometimes mad, sad or scared about the things that he sees around him or on TV. He sometimes sees people hurting each other and being mean to each other. One day he thinks, there has got to be a better way. He decides to go on a journey to find peace and kindness in the world.

4. Ask the children what do they see in their homes, schools and communities? Do they see peace and kindness, or some of the things that worried Gia?

5. Explain that we will be together four times to lean about mindfulness and movement. We will explore (in our imaginations) all the places that Gia visited on his journey: monkey jungle, crocodile swamp, pokey porcupine path, and peaceful porpoise path. When we explore these places we will talk about something called mindfulness.

6. Explain that **mindfulness** is a way of being purposeful about how we pay attention to our thoughts and feelings and what choices we make about who we are and how we act. When we are mindful, we can choose to make our world a more kind and peaceful place.

7. First we will talk about MONKEY JUNGLE. Hold up a picture of a monkey and ask, "What do you notice about monkeys?" Monkeys jump from thing to thing and have a hard time settling down. Sometimes our mind (thoughts and feelings) jump around. Explain and give examples of monkey mind. OR if time permits and children are old enough, make a list of thoughts that jump around in their head. (Perhaps a child is trying to take a math test and his monkey mind is chattering: *I'm worried about my Mom. My teacher is mad at me. I like ice-cream. I'm kinda hungry. I hear a bird chirping. I hope I get picked for basketball. I messed up my math problem. Where's my eraser?*)

8. Explain that monkey mind is normal. It is not bad or good. It just is. It is part of being a kid. However, there are some things that we can do to calm our monkey mind. There are MINDFULNESS TOOLS. First we are going to act like crazy monkey mind and jump around and make noises like monkeys.

Next we are going to practice settling our body and our minds with our new MINDFULNESS TOOLS.

Let the children know exactly how much time is being allotted for the movement part of the activity. Before they start, set up a signal that will let them know when the active part is complete. (E.g. flicker the light).

9. Pick an activity from PART 2 – Calming and mind quieting section. (Pages 13 and 14).
    a. Yoga – the rag doll, and/or quiet mouse.
    b. Belly breathing (optional belly-bags).
    c. 4 count breath.
    d. Guided imagery.
    e. Progressive relaxation.
    f. Focus meditation (optional calm-down jars).

10. As you end the session, tell the children between now and next session, to notice when the monkey is jumping around in their mind (thoughts and feelings) and practice using the calming and quieting mindfulness tools.

11. Establish a formal routine for ending each session. E.g. ring a chime, stand in a circle and bow to each other, or bring your hands with their palms together to the center of your chest (heart center) and say "Namaste'."

Notes and suggestions for session one:

When working with pre-school children focus on the experiential part of the program. For example, it may be enough for children to experience the difference between how a monkey acts (talk about it and do the movement) and how a quiet mouse acts (yoga pose page 23). Is your mind (brain) quieter, when you are a monkey or a mouse? What can you do if you feel like a jumpy monkey (fidgety or like you can't pay attention)? *Take a deep breath and make yourself quiet like a mouse.*

For the monkey movement portion of part 1 have 5-8 yr.-olds move like monkeys and make monkey sounds. Have 9-12 yr.-olds listen to chaotic music and dance. The idea is to create CHAOS.

Session one program enhancers include making belly bags, and calm down jars to be used when practicing the calming and quieting tools. Directions can be found at the back of the book (page 19).

Session two activity: Crocodile Chomp-Down

1. Have the children do the PACE Brain-gym® movements and then sit on the floor in a circle. The PACE Brain-gym® movements are detailed in the back of the book with an explanation of the benefits of the movements. Starting the program with Brain-gym® before being seated will foster a greater ability for the children to be present during the session, and decrease distraction and fidgeting. Tell children Brain-gym® makes them calmer and smarter.

2. Hold up the poster of the child on the path. Remind children that Gia is on a search for peace and kindness in the world. Last session we explored the monkey jungle and the monkey mind.

3. Ask, "Did anyone use the calming or quieting mindfulness tools since last time we met?" Take some time to reinforce the tools and to offer encouragement and appreciation for all efforts.

4. This time we are going to explore the CROCODILE SWAMP and learn about the crocodile chomp down.

5. Hold up a picture of a crocodile and ask, "What do you notice about crocodiles?" Describe how a crocodile chomps down on something and won't let go of it.

6. What happens when we start thinking a thought and we can't get it out of our heads? Talk about how hanging on to troublesome thoughts causes our feelings to intensify (get stronger). Or we can get stuck in a troublesome thought pattern, like a circle that never ends.

7. For example, if I am worried about something and I keep thinking about it, I can get more and more worried or anxious. Use an example from the monkey mind list that they came up with last session –*My teacher is mad at me. I can't do anything right. She likes the other students better than me. I might as well not even try.*

8. If I think about something that makes me mad and I chomp down on it, I can get madder and madder. Ask the children for an example.

9. All thoughts and feelings are ok, but sometimes we have to trick the crocodile in to thinking about something else so he lets the troublesome thoughts go.

10. If the crocodile lets go of the troublesome thought there is more room or space for new thoughts. When we make room for new thoughts, we can focus on helpful or peaceful thoughts. Maybe a helpful thought about how to solve the problem can float in. Maybe a thought of something we like will pop in and help us relax. When we are open to new

thoughts, the feelings we have about the situation become less intense (weaker) rather than more intense (stronger). Remember all feelings are ok to have, but when we get stuck or chomp down on troublesome feelings we can get overwhelmed. We can't figure out how to solve a problem or feel better.

11. Explain the movement portion of the next part of the activity. We are going to act like crocodiles and do some chomping down movements. Demonstrate -arms extended, coming together in a movement that resembles a crocodile's mouth opening and closing. Children can stand and move around the room, or crawl around on their bellies. Ask children to think about how their bodies would move if they were in mucky water. Move in slow motion as if there is resistance. When you give the signal (perhaps a clap or a bell), they have to FREEZE. Before starting the movement, let the children know exactly how much time is being allotted for the movement part of the activity. Set up a signal that will let them know when the movement part is complete. (E.g. flicker the light). This movement and freeze is an ideal way for children to practice mindful awareness by being aware of how their bodies feel and move, and also helps with impulse control. Support all attempts to freeze and remind children to be mindful of each other's space. No chomping down on each other. Keep the time for this activity very short.

12. Have all the children rejoin you in "the swamp" and sit in a circle. You may need to ask them to put their "chompers" in their laps, so they can focus on the next MINDFULNESS TOOL you are going to teach them.

13. Pick an activity from PART 2 – Thought stopping and reframing (page 15).
    a. STOP sign (stop, take a breath, observe, and proceed).
    b. STAR – stop, take a deep breath, and relax.
    c. Positive affirmations: *I am safe, I am calm, I am loved, I belong, I make good choices.*
    d. Touchstone (optional have them choose a stone or shell).
    e. Sanctuary (special place).

14. As you end the session, tell the children between now and next session, to notice when they are chomping down on troublesome thoughts and practice using the thought stopping and reframing mindfulness tools.

15. Transition to your ending routine.

Notes and Suggestions: When working with pre-school children, gage their capacity for understanding the cognitive concepts and adjust accordingly. Because pre-school children learn through experience it may be enough to have them do the crocodile movements and then focus on how they can Stop, Take a deep breath And Relax. Perhaps have the children pretend to be crocodiles sleeping in the sun and provide a brief guided visualization. *You are safe and warm, and oh so very still. Your eye lids close down over your eyes and you feel your body relax as it soaks up the warm sun (have the children lay still for 1-2 minutes) You keep the warm and relaxed feeling with you as you begin to stretch and wake up.*

Notes and Suggestions Continued: An alternative activity for number 11 page 10- is to have children do an open and close motion with their thumb extended and fingers together (like a claw). Move the hand up and down the arms, across the shoulders and up and down the legs. This is a sensory experience for children and helps them feel grounded in their physical body. Compare the motion to a "chomping" and talk about how feeling the sensations in our bodies can help take our mind off troublesome thoughts.

Session three activity: Pokey Porcupine

1. Have the children do the PACE Brain-gym® movements and then sit on the floor in a circle. The PACE Brain-gym® movements are detailed in the back of the book with an explanation of the benefits of the movements. Starting the program with Brain-gym® before being seated will foster a greater ability for the children to be present during the session, and decrease distraction and fidgeting. Tell the children Brain-gym® makes them calmer and smarter.

2. Hold up the poster of the child on the path. Remind the children that Gia is on a search for peace and kindness in the world. During the first session we explored the monkey jungle and the monkey mind. During the second session we explored the crocodile swamp and practiced stopping our thoughts, letting go, and making room for more helpful thoughts.

3. Ask, "Did anyone use the thought stopping or reframing mindfulness tools since last time we met?" Take some time to reinforce the tools and to offer encouragement and appreciation for all efforts.

4. This time we are going to explore the POKEY PORCUPINE path. Explain that the boy on the poster has come to a fork in the road. He has to decide if he wants to go down a pokey porcupine path or a peaceful porpoise path. We will talk about the porcupine path this session and the porpoise path next time. For now let's think about, "Do you ever go down the pokey porcupine path? How can we all notice when we are heading that way?" Once we know more about the two paths we can decide which path is going to make Gia's life better. You can make choices, too in real life. Which path might make your life better? Where is Gia going to find peace and kindness?

5. Show a picture of a porcupine. What do you notice about porcupines? Talk about how the porcupine can protect itself with its quills and can hurt others with its quills.

6. What if our thoughts are like porcupine quills. Could we think, say or do something hurtful to others or even to ourselves? If I say, "I am so stupid." I am poking myself with a quill. If I say, "You are so stupid." I am poking you with a quill. If someone says or does something hurtful to us, we sometimes want to retaliate (get them back).

7. Ask for examples from the students, or give an example. What if the teacher says, "Johnny I am talking and you are not listening. What is the matter with you?" Is that hurtful? Helpful?

    Now Johnny can say to himself,
    "There is something the matter with me. I can never pay attention." Is that helpful or hurtful?
    Johnny can say, "I hate my teacher. She always picks on me." Is that helpful or hurtful?

8. Have them think about times they may say hurtful things silently or out loud about themselves or others. Tell the students that we will think about more helpful ways to speak to ourselves and others, when we go down the peaceful porpoise path.

9. Have students stand up and create a personal space zone- an imaginary circle around their body that no one can enter. Talk about what it means to have a personal space zone. You can choose who can and cannot come close to you.

10. Have students work in pairs – face each other and step back about five feet. Have one student be stationary and decide how close he would want the other student to come if he/she were a pokey thought or pokey porcupine. Have the second student start moving toward the stationary student. When the moving student is close enough have the stationary student put his/her hand up to indicate stop and say in an assertive voice, "That is close enough. I am not interested in pokes today!"

11. Remind students that not all pokey thoughts come from others. It is really important not to poke themselves with their own words. If they think a pokey thought, they can say "I am not listening to any pokey thoughts today, thank you!" (Remind them of the thought stopping technique that was taught last session.)

12. Have children practice zipping up their personal space zone. When someone says something hurtful to you, you can zip up your space and protect yourself. You can also make a choice not to be hurtful back.

13. Have each child stand stationary with their feet slightly apart. Tell the children to think about the energy (space) that is right around their body. Think about zipping up that space for protection – like creating an invisible cocoon. Bend toward the floor, moving hands and arms in a swooping motion, bring the palms of the hands together making a zipping motion up your front (as if there were a big zipper from your feet to your chin). Pretend to zip the space as you come to a standing position and lift your hands with palms together over your head and then bring them to the center of your chest. Tell children they can zip-up anytime they are feeling the need for protection.

14. Shift gears from zipping up to releasing energy. Tell children you are going to learn a new MINDFULNESS TOOL to help them release energy when they are feeling pokey.

15. Pick an activity from PART TWO – energy release activities (page 17).
    a. Yoga – Cat/Cow.
    b. Shake it off.
    c. Scribble it out.

16. As you end the session, ask the children between now and next session, to notice when they are on the pokey path: 1) being poked by another person, 2) poking another person, 3) poking themselves. They can use the zip up method for protection, the energy release mindfulness tools to get rid of pokey feelings and/or any of the tools we learned for calming (session 1) and thought stopping or reframing (session 2).

17. Transition to your ending routine.

Notes and Suggestions:

When working with pre-school children focus on the experiential part of the program. For example, it may be enough for children to experience the difference between when they are feeling like a pokey porcupine and when they are not. They might be pokey (grumpy) if they are hungry or tired, or bored. They can stop themselves from poking others by shaking it off, scribbling it out, or zipping it up. If someone is going to poke them they can say "STOP" in an assertive voice. Have them practice STOP as directed on page 15.

Session four activity: Peaceful Porpoise

1. Have the children do the PACE Brain-gym® movements and then sit on the floor in a circle. The PACE Brain-gym® movements are detailed in the back of the book with an explanation of the benefits of the movements. Starting the program with Brain-gym® before being seated will foster a greater ability for the children to be present during the session, and decrease distraction and fidgeting. Tell children Brain-gym® makes them calmer and smarter.

2. Hold up the poster of the child on the path. Remind children that Gia is on a search for peace and kindness in the world. At the first session we explored the monkey jungle and the monkey mind. At the second session we explored the crocodile swamp and practiced stopping our thoughts, letting go, and making room for more helpful thoughts. Last week we discussed being on a pokey porcupine path and how to be aware of our pokiness, how to protect and be kinder to ourselves, and how to be less pokey with others.

3. Ask children if they want to share any of the experiences they noticed as they were being more aware of the pokey path. Briefly process the answers and move the conversation to the peaceful porpoise lesson.

4. This time we are going to explore the PEACEFUL PORPOISE path. This is the path that leads to peace and kindness and is the path that Gia has been searching for.

5. Show a picture of a porpoise. What do you notice about porpoises? Focus on how they swim in schools and how they are very intelligent and peaceful creatures. They cooperate and solve problems peacefully.

6. Upset or troublesome thoughts and feelings give us a clue that there is a problem. BUT they are not good for helping us solve problems and cooperate with others. When we notice a troublesome thought or feeling we can decide to let the thought or feeling pass through (not chomp down on it, or get pokey about it). We can DECIDE to stay calm and peaceful so we can solve the problem in a kind and peaceful way.

7. If you practice mindfulness tools, it is easier to stay calm when you are troubled or upset. Today we are going to learn a very cool MINDFULNESS TOOL that helps you BE GRrr-8. When you make a figure 8 in the air and follow it with your eyes, it helps your brain calm down and become more peaceful. When your brain is more

peaceful, your body begins to relax, too. Think about how a porpoise swims up and down and around, floating and swimming peacefully in the water.

8. Do a figure 8 motion in the air with your index finger several times and have the children be as still as they can, and watch your finger move with their eyes only.

9. Now have the children use their own finger to draw a figure 8 in the air. Have them do the motion several times and watch with their eyes only.

10. Teach the children this phrase, "When I am upset or troubled, I can choose to be GR-8 and solve the problem peacefully."

11. Have the children hook their thumbs together and say the phrase as they engage both hands in the figure 8 movement. Do two or three figure 8 movements and then bring the hands with palms together to the center of the chest (heart center.)

12. Ask the children, "Why do you think we end with our hands by our heart?" Process and suggest that we are all connected heart to heart.

13. When Gia traveled to the end of the peaceful porpoise path, he felt peaceful, calm and a sense of kindness (compassion) toward himself and other people, and all living creatures.

14. We are going to learn a new MINDFULNESS TOOL to practice heart connections.

15. Pick an activity from PART 2- Mindfulness tools- heart connections. (page 17)
    a. Read – The Invisible String by Patrice Karst
    b. Heart connections with yarn.
    c. Yoga- Saluting the Sun

16. As you end the session, remind the children that this is the last session of mindfulness and movement. Hold up the poster and say to the children, "Just like Gia, we went searching and exploring all these areas along the path looking for a kind and peaceful world. The kind and peaceful place is with us all the time. There is a kind and peaceful place inside each of us. When we practice mindfulness that peace and kindness gets stronger and stronger. We can make a kinder and more peaceful world around us, just by being mindful."

17. You may choose to use your established routine for ending the session, or do something special for closure. E.g. Circle with feet touching and/or Heartfelt comments to each group member. (Find directions in PART 2- heart connection closure page 18)

Congratulate the children and yourself for a job well done! Namasté.

Notes and Suggestions:

When working with pre-school children focus on the experiential part of the program. For example, it may be enough for children to pretend to be a peaceful porpoise swimming in water and practice the statement and hand motions to, "I am GR-8." Drawing figure 8's in shaving cream, sand or on paper is a wonderful way to integrate the right and left hemisphere of the brain and is very beneficial in calming.

To learn more about the integration of the brain through the use of movement read Smart Moves: Why Learning is Not All in Your Head, by Carla Hannaford. 2nd Edition, Carla Hannaford, Great River Books, Salt Lake City, Utah, 2005.

Begin Each Session with Brain-gym®

P.A.C.E. stands for **Positive, Active, Clear, and Energetic**. There are four parts to it.

1. **Energetic-** Take a drink of water.

Water makes up 76% of body weight. It ionizes salt, increasing electrical potential across membranes. It is essential for protein formation and function of nerve nets. It increases oxygen uptake by hemoglobin.

2. **Clear** – Take the right hand and place the thumb and forefinger in the indents right below the clavicle bones. Gently rub the "brain buttons" with the thumb and forefinger. Rubbing the "brain buttons" will clear the mind and the brain will be ready for new information. Place the left hand over the naval while continuing to rub the "brain buttons." Take a couple of deep breaths and feel the belly expand and deflate.

The buttons are located above the carotid arteries, which supply fresh oxygenated blood to the brain, and K-27 points for lung/brain function. The hand on the navel brings attention to the body's gravitational center.

3. **Active** - While standing, lift the left knee and touch it with the right hand. Next, lift the right knee and touch it with the left hand. Continue to repeat the back and forth motion. This is the "Cross Crawl" motion.

The Cross Crawl activates both hemispheres of the neo-cortex simultaneously – motor and sensory cortexes of parietal and frontal lobes. Done slowly, it activates the vestibular system for balance.

4. **Positive – Hook-ups** - Sit down and place the tip of the tongue on the roof of the mouth, at the same time touch the fingertips of the right hand to the fingertips of the left hand. This is called "Hook-ups"

The hook-up motion activates sensory and motor cortexes in both hemispheres of the cerebrum simultaneously. The tongue connects the limbic system and frontal lobes.

BRAIN GYM® is a registered trademark of the Educational Kinesiology Foundation and is an educational program, which uses simple movements to enhance learning abilities in children and adults. The Program was developed by Paul E. Dennison, Ph.D., an expert in child motor development. It is based upon 80 years of research by educational therapists, developmental optometrists, and other developmental specialists.

PART 2- Mindfulness and Movement Tools

Calming (relaxation) and mind quieting activities.

Choose at least one of these activities to use with session one, and reiterate and practice as often as possible.

1. Yoga –rag- doll and quiet mouse (Instructions for the yoga pose can be found on page 18).

2. Belly breathing (optional belly-bags).
    Instructions: Have the children lie on the floor with one hand on their belly and one hand by their side. If choosing to use the belly bag, the child will place the belly bag on their belly and hold it in place with one hand. Instruct children to inhale, pushing air into the belly and feeling the belly inflate. Instruct children to exhale, releasing air and deflating the belly. Repeat 3-5 times. If choosing to use the belly bag, have children watch the bag move up and down on their belly while the breath moves in and out.

3. Four count breath.
    Instructions: Have the children inhale through their nose while the facilitator slowly counts 1, 2, 3, 4. Have the children hold their breath while the facilitator slowly counts 1, 2, 3, 4. Have children breathe out through the nose while the facilitator slowly counts 1, 2, 3, 4, 5, 6. Have children hold the breath at the top while the facilitator counts 1, 2. Begin the entire process again with inhaling to the count of 4. Repeat 3-4 times.

4. Guided imagery.
    Instructions: Explain to the children what guided imagery is. It is a way for them to relax their bodies and minds, by listening to a story and using their imaginations to create an experience.

    Have the children sit or lie down and read the following paragraph slowly. Pause as appropriate for children to listen to the words, process the words and feel the sensations.

Sit comfortably and close your eyes. Breathe in deeply and breathe out deeply, breathe in, breathe out, breathe in, breathe out. Notice your breathing now as it goes back to normal. Let your arms and legs become heavy and feel your body relax. Pretend that you are in the ocean. Pretend that you are a beautiful tropical fish. The clothes that you are wearing turn in to beautiful bright colored scales. Think about swimming in an ocean. The ocean water is warm. The ocean is very quiet and peaceful. Look around with your imagination. What else do you see? Maybe you see plants, colored sand, sea shells? Some fish swim very quickly, moving from place to place. Some fish move very slowly, gliding along in the water and floating. You decide to slow down and float. You are effortlessly floating in the warm salty water. Your body is completely relaxed as you watch the fish and plants around you (pause for a few moments and let the children relax and imagine floating). You have had a wonderful and relaxing time being a fish. You decide to keep the feeling of relaxation with you when you change back in to a boy or girl. I will count backward from 10 to 1. When I reach 1, you can flutter your eyes open and come back to land. 10,9,8,7,6,5,4,3,2,1 (count slowly). Open your eyes and wiggle your hands and feet.

5. Progressive relaxation.

    Instructions: Have children lie down and close their eyes or lower their lids and focus on breathing. As you give the cues below, have the children focus on completing each action when directed. After giving the command to tighten each area of the body, silently count to 3 before giving the cue to relax. This brief pause allows the children to notice the difference between the sensations of tight and relaxed and builds body awareness.

    - Tighten feet and toes, then relax
    - Tighten legs, then relax
    - Tighten belly, then relax
    - Tighten hands and arms, then relax
    - Move to tightening shoulders by bringing shoulders to the ears and then releasing them down, and end with scrunching the face and then releasing.

    Once each area of the body has been tightened and released allow the children to lie quietly and notice how relaxed their body feels. After a couple of minutes have children gently shake their bodies awake and move to the next activity.

6. Focus meditation. Purchase glitter wands, or if time permits have children make their own calm-down jars. (See references and resources for glitter wand purchase information and page 19 for instructions on how to make calm down jars).

Instructions: Instruct children to sit in a circle. Each child will need a glitter wand or calm down jar. Have children close their eyes and slowly take 2 deep breaths. As they open their eyes have them gently turn the glitter wand or calm down jar upside down. Instruct children to watch and notice the glitter as it falls to the bottom. At the same time have them notice how calm their minds are becoming and how their breath is moving slowly in and out. Allow the focused meditation to continue for a minute or two. Sit quietly for a few seconds after all the glitter has settled.

Thought stopping – reframing activities. Choose at least one of these activities to use with session two, and reiterate and practice as often as possible.

1. STOP sign - stop, take a breath, observe, and proceed.

    Instructions: Have children stand and imitate the following movements as the lead facilitator demonstrates: 1) STOP- hold one hand up, palm facing out like a stop sign, 2) Take a breath- inhale deeply with hand on heart and belly, 3) Observe- exhale and bring hands to eyes, fingers form circles as if looking through binoculars, 4) Proceed- bring one hand waist height palm up and pretend the two fingers of the other hand are walking across the palm.

2. STAR – stop, take a deep breath, and relax.

    Instructions: Have children stand and imitate the following movements as the lead facilitator demonstrates: 1) STOP- stand motionless with hands to side, 2) Take a deep breath - move hands to the belly and heart and inhale deeply, 3) Relax- exhale while lightly shake body like a rag doll with floppy arms releasing energy from the fingertips.

3. Positive affirmations.
    Instructions: Have children sit in a circle with hands in their laps. Sit in the circle with the children and explain that you are going to say same positive (nice, kind, powerful) statements. Instruct children to repeat (with conviction) the statements you are saying. While they are saying the statements, ask them to think about what they mean, not just say the words. Say the following statements, pausing between each one so the children can repeat them. This is called call and return. You say the statement, they return the statement: *I am safe, I am calm, I am loved, I belong, I make good choices.* Feel free to add statements that are relevant to your group (optional say the statements in different ways: a soft voice, loud voice, proud voice etc.).

4. Touchstone (optional have them choose a stone or shell as explained on page 19)

5. Sanctuary (special place)

   Instructions: Explain that a sanctuary is a peaceful place that can be created in someone's imagination. It is a feel good place that is always safe. Sometimes children remember a real place they have been, other times children create a new place from their own imaginations.

   Have children sit or lie down and ask them to listen to your voice and relax into their sanctuary.

   Read the following paragraph and pause periodically for children to create images and sensations as you go:

   Close your eyes and take a deep breath. As you breathe out begin to imagine a place that feels good and safe to you. This may be a place you have visited in real life, or a place that you create with your own imagination. This is a feel good place, where you feel safe. It might be outdoors, maybe a beach, or a forest, or a park. It is up to you where you would like to be. This is your safe place. It might be indoors, a special place filled with things you enjoy or love. You are creating this place. (pause) It is your special place. Look around. What do you see in this place? (pause) What colors, shapes or objects? (pause) Is there anyone there with you? Is there a person or animal you want to include in your safe place? Or maybe you are there alone. (pause) It is your place. You are in charge of who comes and goes. (pause) What do you smell in this place? (pause) What do you hear? Maybe there are lots of sounds. Maybe it is quiet. (pause) Just listen and notice what you hear. (pause) Maybe you hear wind, water or music. Can you imagine touching the things around you? What might they feel like? Are they soft or hard, cold or warm, rough or smooth? Just notice in this place you are feeling calm, relaxed, safe, warm, loved and accepted. This is your special place. This is your sanctuary. You can go to this place in your imagination anytime. This safe place is always with you. As you look around one last time, begin to notice your body and breathing, open your eyes and come back to this room.

   If time permits you may ask children to volunteer to tell you about their sanctuary.

Energy release activities. Choose at least one of these activities to use with session three, and reiterate and practice as often as possible.

1. Yoga –cat/cow (page 18).
2. Shake it off.
   Instructions: Have children stand and shake their entire body from head to toe or play music such as Taylor Swift's song, *Shake it Off,* if working with children 9-12 yrs.-old.
3. Scribble it out.
   Instructions: Have each child choose a sturdy piece of paper and 2-3 crayons (broken FAT crayons are best, brown paper bags work great as paper). Tell the children they can scribble whatever shapes and forms they would like on the paper. The idea is to scribble without thinking about what they are making. If they want to express pent up energy or strong emotions they can scribble hard.

Heart connection activities. Choose at least one of these activities to use with session four, and reiterate and practice as often as possible.

1. Read – The Invisible String, by Patrice Karst
2. Heart connections with yarn.
   Instructions: Have children sit in a circle facing each other. You will be creating a yarn network (like a spider web connecting all the children to each other). Begin by handing a ball of yarn to the first child. The child should choose someone across from him/her, and give them a positive message (E.g. You are kind. You are a nice friend. You are helpful. I like your ___). After they state the positive message, they will hold on to one end of the yarn and hand (gently toss) the yarn ball to the child they have given the positive affirmation to. The yarn will unravel. There will be a string of yarn connecting one child to the other. Continue the activity until all children are holding a piece of yarn and are connected in the circle.

3. Yoga- Saluting the Sun (page 19).

Heart connection– closure. Choose at least one of these activities or do both to close session four and the program.

1. Circle with feet touching.
    Instructions: Have children sit in a circle with legs extended and feet touching (like the spokes of a wagon-wheel). Ask children to be still and notice the connection that they feel with all the other children in the group.

    This is a connection they will carry with them even when the group is no longer meeting every week (this is best done barefoot or in sock feet and when toe wiggling and giggling are encouraged).

2. Heartfelt comments to each group member.
    Instructions: Have children focus on one group member at a time and take turns saying something positive, affirmative (nice) about that person. They might choose to begin the statement with one of these open ended sentence starters, or choose their own starter: I like the way you____. One thing I will miss about you is _____. One thing I want you to know is _____.

Yoga Poses

The Rag Doll:

1. Stand straight and tall.
2. Bend over at the hips, keeping your weight even on both feet.
3. Let your head and arms hang limply down toward the floor.
4. Pretend you are a rag-doll swaying side to side.

The Quiet Mouse:

1. Kneel on a mat (or a towel, or rug) with your knees and feet together. Your toes should point backward.
2. Lean back on your heels, sitting tall with your shoulders relaxed.
3. Breathe out slowly and lower your body until your head touches the floor.
4. Stretch your arms out in front of you, or bring them close in to your sides.
5. Each time you breathe out, let your chest get closer to your knees.
6. Keep your shoulders relaxed.
7. Picture in your mind that you are getting as quiet as a mouse.

The Cat/Cow:

1. Kneel on all fours with your palms flat on the floor.
2. As you breath out, hollow your back, keeping your arms straight (sway back –like an old cow). Then inhale.
3. On the next out-breath, arch your back (like a Halloween cat). Then inhale.
4. On the next out-breath, come back to the original neutral position.

Saluting the Sun:

1. Stand tall with legs and feet together.
2. Take a deep breath in.
3. Reach arms above the head with finger tips touching.
4. Exhale – bending forward (as if bowing to the sun) arms stretch out wide and then down towards the floor.
5. Inhale – bring hands to knees, flat back.
6. Exhale- bend forward toward the floor.
7. Take a big breath in.
8. Slowly stand up bringing hands overhead palms touching.
9. Bring hands to the middle of the chest (heart center).

(Adapted from Shapario, 2009)

Optional Mindfulness Props

Calm-down jars (optional for lesson one)

You will need:

- A plastic jar with a cover (a small mayonnaise jar or a 12 oz. water bottle work well)
- Warm water
- Colored glitter glue
- A few colored beads or extra glitter (optional)
- Superglue

Fill the jar with warm water. Leave a couple of inches or "room" at the top. Squirt 2-3 ounces of glitter glue in the water. Drop the beads and extra glitter in the water (optional). Close the lid tightly and shake until the glitter glue dissolves. Superglue the lid of the jar in place (should be done by an adult).

Keep the calm down jar in a quiet space. A child can choose to use the jar as a calming aid. Instruct the child, that when they are feeling troublesome emotions they can: go to the quiet space, gently shake the calm down jar (turn it this way and that), think calming thoughts as they watch the glitter in the jar settle down. Notice that the upset feelings or monkey mind settles down as the glitter floats to the bottom of the jar.

Belly-bags (Bean-bags - optional for lesson one)

You will need:

- a clean child size sock (for each child)
- one cup of dried beans per child (depending on the size of the sock)
- one rubber band per child

Scoop the dried beans into the sock until it is ½ full. Place the rubber-band securely around the sock directly above the beans ½ way up. Roll any extra sock over the bean-bag portion of the sock. Make sure the beans are secured in the sock to avoid beans leaking out or children taking them out. Instruct the child to place the belly-bag on their belly while they are practicing mindful breathing. They can watch the bean-bag move up and down on their belly as they inhale and exhale.

Touchstone (optional for lesson two)

A touchstone is a small item, like a stone or shell that a child can hold in their hand. The child holds the item in their hand while in a state of relaxation. The item becomes a bridge to relaxation when the child feels stressed or overwhelmed during everyday activities.

References and Resources:

Books:

Hannaford, Carla, 2005, *Smart Moves: Why Learning Is Not All In Your Head.*, 2nd edition, Great River Books, Salt lake City, Utah.

Karst, Patrice, 2000, *The Invisible String*, DeVorss & Company Publishers, California.

Shapiro, Lawrence E. and Sprague, Robin K., 2009, *The Relaxation and Stress Reduction Workbook for Kids*, Instant Help Press, California

Siegel, Daniel J., 2011, *The Whole-Brain Child*, Bantam Books, New York

Resources:

Glitter wands can be purchased at http://www.officeplayground.com

Association for Mindfulness in Education www.mindfulnessinschools.org

http://timryan.house.gov/press-release/congressman-tim-ryan-introduces-academic-social-and-emotional-learning-act-0

For information on:

- Mindfulness and Movement for Children© workshops
  - Mindfulness and Movement Implementation training

Contact:

Michele Tryon –

michele@micheletryon.com

www.micheletryon.com

Marsha Engle –

mengle@themindfullivinginstitute.org

Marsha.j.engle@gmail.com

Gia begins his journey

Monkey Jungle

Crocodile Swamp

Pokey Porcupine Path

Peaceful Porpoise Path

Gia's Journey to Find Peace and Kindness

Made in the USA
Middletown, DE
23 December 2016